W9-AAM-170

Animal Lives

BEES AND WASPS

Sally Morgan

QEB Publishing

Copyright © QEB Publishing, Inc. 2006

First published in the United States by
QEB Publishing, Inc.
23062 La Cadena Drive
Laguna Hills, CA 92653

www.qeb-publishing.com
Reprinted in 2007

All rights reserved. No part of this publication may be reproduced, stored in a retrieval system, or transmitted in any form or by any means, electronic, mechanical, photocopying, recording, or otherwise, without the prior permission of the publisher, nor be otherwise circulated in any form of binding or cover other than that in which it is published and without a similar condition being imposed on the subsequent purchaser.

Library of Congress Control Number:
2005911033

ISBN 978 1 59566 492 1

Written by Sally Morgan
Designed by Jonathan Vipond
Editor Hannah Ray
Picture Researcher Joanne Forrest Smith

Publisher Steve Evans
Art Director Zeta Davies
Editorial Director Jean Coppendale

Printed and bound in China

Picture Credits

Key: t=top, b=bottom, l=left, r=right, c=center, FC=front cover

Ardea/Brian Bevan 23, /Steve Hopkin 12, /John Mason 30br; **Corbis**/Ralph A Clevenger 14–15, /George D Lepp 21, /Joe McDonald 7, /Lynda Richardson 8–9, 25; **Ecoscene**/Martin Beames 11bl, /Robert Pickett 10, 19br, 26, 31tr, /Robin Williams 1, 29tr /Ken Wilson 15; **FLPA**/Nigel Cattlin 11tr, 17, /Treat Davidson 27, /Ernie Janes 18–19, /Silvestris Fotoservice 22, /Jurgen & Christine Sohns 24; **NHPA**/Anthony Bannister 16, /N A Callow 28–29, /Stephen Dalton 5, 6, 13, 20, 30tl, FC, /N A Callow 4.

Words in **bold** are explained in the Glossary on page 31.

Contents

Bees and wasps 4
Types of bee and wasp 6
Where can you find bees and wasps? 8
Eggs and larvae 10
Colonies 12
Building homes 14
Solitary wasps 16
Bee and wasp senses 18
Bee and wasp flight 20
Bee and wasp food 22
Who eats bees and wasps? 24
Bee and wasp communication 26
Bees and wasps under threat 28
Life cycle of a honeybee 30
Glossary 31
Index 32

Bees and wasps

Bees and wasps are brightly colored **insects**, and most of them sting! Insects are invertebrates, which means they do not have a backbone. An adult insect has three body parts: a head, a middle part called the **thorax**, and a part at the end called the **abdomen**. They also have three pairs of legs.

All wasps and bees, such as this honeybee, have two pairs of wings.

Bee or wasp?

Bees and wasps can be identified by the narrow waist between the thorax and the abdomen, something not found in other insects. It can be difficult to tell a bee from a wasp because they look similar, but bees have a hairy body and legs, while wasps have far fewer hairs.

Bee and wasp fact

The honeybee was introduced to America by the first European colonists. Native Americans called it "White Man's Fly."

The common wasp has bright yellow and black stripes across its abdomen.

Changing appearance

There are four stages in a bee or wasp's life: egg, **larva**, **pupa**, and adult. At each stage, the bee or wasp looks very different.

Types of bee and wasp

There may be as many as 200,000 different types of bees and wasps, but only about 50,000 have been fully identified. The smallest are tiny **parasitic** wasps, just a millimeter or so in length, while the largest are hornets.

Hornets can grow up to 1.25 in. (30 mm) in length.

Bees

Honeybees and bumblebees are the most common types of bees. They are **social** bees and live in large groups. However, most other species of bees are **solitary** and live on their own.

Bee and wasp fact

Many people think that hornets are dangerous, but the hornet is a shy insect and is unlikely to sting unless attacked.

Wasps

Wasps can also be divided into social and solitary types. Social wasps include the common wasps, paper wasps, and hornets. The potter, digger, and parasitic wasps are all solitary wasps.

Paper wasps chew up wood to make a sort of papier mâché, which they use to build their nests.

Where can you find bees and wasps?

Bees and wasps are found all over the world. Honeybees, bumblebees, and other types of bees that feed on **nectar** are found in **habitats** where there are plenty of flowers, for example in meadows, grasslands, woodlands, and rainforests. They are also regular visitors to gardens and parks. Wasps live in the same habitats as bees, and are also found in deserts.

Beekeeping

The common honeybee originally came from Asia, but it has now been introduced into most countries of the world. This species is kept by beekeepers because the bees make much more honey than they can eat themselves, which means the leftover honey can be harvested by the beekeepers.

Beekeepers have to wear protective clothing so they do not get stung when they open the hive.

Bee and wasp fact

The Africanized honeybee is unlike other honeybees, because it is quite aggressive and will sting even when it is not disturbed.

Eggs and larvae

Bees and wasps lay eggs. A bee egg is just 0.05 in. (1.3 mm) long, about half the size of a grain of rice. A few days after the egg is laid, a larva hatches out. The larva looks like a small, white caterpillar. All the larvae do is eat and grow bigger and bigger. Honeybee larvae eat **pollen** and honey, while wasp larvae eat other animals such as small insects and caterpillars.

Honeybee larvae live in cells inside the hive.

Bee and wasp fact

A queen bee lays one egg per minute, day and night.

These are the pupae of honeybees. Their bodies are changing to become adults.

This honeybee is coming out of its pupal cell.

Metamorphosis

When the larva is fully grown, it becomes a pupa. It is during this stage that the body of the larva changes into that of an adult bee or wasp. This change is called **metamorphosis**. It takes about eight to ten days before the adult insect emerges from the pupa.

Colonies

A queen bee's body is much longer than the bodies of other bees.

Social bees and wasps live together in large groups called colonies. Each member of the colony has a particular job to do.

In a honeybee colony, there are three types of bees: queens, drones, and workers. There is usually a single queen. She is the largest bee and lays all the eggs. Drones are large male bees that have no sting. Their only job is to **mate** with the queen.

Workers

The majority of bees are worker bees. They are small, busy bees. The young workers are "house bees" who care for the queen, remove waste, build the nest, and guard the nest's entrance. They also keep the nest cool by fanning their wings. "Nurse bees" feed and take care of the larvae, while the older worker bees, called foragers, are responsible for collecting nectar, pollen, and water.

Bee and Wasp fact

A rich food called royal jelly is made in the nurse bee's head. If this jelly is fed to a larva that is less than three days old, it develops into a new queen.

These worker honeybees are filling cells with the food they have collected from flowers.

Building homes

Honeybees and social wasps are expert home builders. They build complex nests in which they lay their eggs. Honeybees make their home from wax, while wasps chew wood into a pulp which they use to build their nest.

Bees' nests

A bees' nest contains hanging structures called combs, which are made of wax. Each comb is made up of units called cells. The cells contain eggs, larvae, pupae, and stockpiles of pollen and honey. As the nest gets larger, it includes more and more combs.

The walls of the cells are thin but can support many times their own weight.

Bee and wasp fact

Honeybees produce beeswax from the underside of their abdomens. They have to eat 17 lb. (8 kg) of honey to make a pound (half a kilogram) of beeswax.

These pictures show the building of a wasps' nest. It starts with a stalk hanging from a ceiling or overhead support.

Wasps' nests

A wasps' nest is started by the queen, who lays a few eggs that hatch into worker bees. The workers build the cone-shaped nest and it gradually gets larger, often reaching the size of a soccer ball. The entrance hole is at the bottom.

Solitary wasps

Not all bees and wasps live in groups. Many are solitary insects that live alone and feed themselves. They nest in tiny holes in walls and trees, or build their own tiny nests.

Potter wasps

The nest of the potter wasp is a tiny pot of clay. The female wasp builds the pot, lays an egg, and then kills a caterpillar or a spider, which she places in the pot beside her egg. Then she seals up the pot. The larva hatches out of the egg and feeds on the body of the caterpillar or spider.

This female potter wasp has paralyzed a caterpillar with her sting.

Bee and wasp fact

The fairyfly, a tiny parasitic wasp, swims underwater to find beetles' eggs in which to lay its own eggs.

Parasitic wasps

Parasitic wasps are small wasps that lay their eggs in the bodies of other animals. They usually have a very long, needle-like structure at the end of their abdomen. This isn't a sting. It is called an ovipositor and is used for laying eggs. Parasitic wasps use it to inject their eggs inside a **host insect**.

This parasitic wasp is laying its eggs in the body of an aphid.

Bee and wasp senses

Bees and wasps have five eyes. Two are large, compound eyes and three are small, simple eyes. The simple eyes can tell if it is bright or dark, while the compound eyes are good for seeing in color. Bees and wasps can see a wider range of colors than humans can. For example, bees cannot see the color red very well, but they can see **ultraviolet**. This means that many flowers look different to them.

Bee and wasp fact

Scientists have trained a type of parasitic wasp to find buried landmines by using their sense of smell.

Bees and wasps use their **antennae** to detect scents in the air.

Ultraviolet

Many flowers have ultraviolet lines on their petals, which guide bees to the nectar inside the flower. These lines can only be seen by humans when viewed under a special ultraviolet light.

A dandelion is a yellow flower, but it looks very different when seen under ultraviolet light.

Bee and wasp flight

Honeybees can fly at speeds of up to 19 mph (30 km/h). They usually fly only a few miles from their nest in search of food. However, it has been known for bees to travel as far as 9 mi. (14 km).

On warm sunny days, bees can be seen flying from flower to flower in search of food.

Bee and wasp fact

Honeybees flap their wings more than 230 times per second. It is this rapid flapping that creates the buzzing sound of the bee.

Wings

Bees and wasps have two pairs of thin, see-through wings. The front pair of wings is larger than the hind (back) pair. The hind wings cling to the front pair using tiny hooks, so the two sets of wings move as if they were one.

Buzz pollinators

Blue-banded bees found in Australia are known as buzz pollinators. They use a special technique to get the pollen from flowers. They hold onto the flowers and **vibrate** with a loud buzzing sound. The vibration causes the pollen to drop from the flower and onto the bee's back.

Carpenter bees, such as this one, are also buzz pollinators.

Bee and wasp food

Bees visit flowers to collect nectar and pollen. They have a long tongue with a "honey spoon" at the end, which they use to sip up the nectar.

Back at the nest, the nectar is passed to other worker bees who store it in cells. The water evaporates from the nectar, leaving a thick, honey syrup. The bees feed on the honey during the winter.

Bees gather pollen and put it into pollen baskets on their legs.

Wasp food

Like wasp larvae, most adult wasps are meat eaters and feed on other insects and spiders. However, they will also feed on nectar and on juice from fallen fruits.

Bee and wasp fact

Wasps are a friend of the gardener because they feed on garden pests such as aphids, whiteflies, and houseflies, which damage plants.

These wasps are feeding on the sugary juices of a plum.

Who eats bees and wasps?

Bees and wasps are **preyed** upon by a variety of animals. Some get caught up in spiders' webs while others are eaten by birds, such as bee-eaters. Honey badgers are **predators**, too. Although its name suggests that the badger eats honey, it actually raids bees' nests to eat the larvae.

The bee-eater catches the bee and then hammers it on a branch to remove the sting before eating it.

Warning colors

Bees and wasps that sting are usually brightly colored. These colors act as a warning to predators.

Bee and wasp fact

Bee stings can be treated with baking soda. Vinegar is good for wasp stings.

Most bees only sting to protect themselves or their nest.

When a bee wants to sting a predator, it pushes its sting through the skin of the attacker and pumps in a poison. When the bee pulls away, the sting is left in the predator's body. This injures the bee and it soon dies. A wasp can pull out its sting after it has injected its poison, and so it survives after stinging an attacker.

Bee and wasp communication

Bees and wasps communicate with each other all the time, mainly by using smells. The insects release scent chemicals called pheromones. These help male and female bees and wasps to find each other. Scents are also used to send warnings and to help worker bees from the same nest to identify each other.

These wasps come from the same nest and recognize each other by smell.

Bee and wasp fact

Never kill a wasp near its nest! Dying wasps release a smell that alerts other wasps. They will come to defend the dying wasp within 15 seconds.

The honeybees' dance takes place inside the nest.

Dancing bees

When a honeybee finds a good source of food, it returns to the nest to tell the others. It does a dance to show where the food can be found and how far away it is. If the bee walks around in a loop, it means the food is close by. If the food is farther away, the bee does a "waggle dance." It walks in a figure eight, wiggling its abdomen, and this tells the other bees how far and in which direction to fly.

Bees and wasps under threat

Honeybees and common wasps are common insects. However, some species are endangered and are at risk of becoming **extinct**.

One of the reasons for their decline is a loss of habitat. Also, farmers use pesticides to kill insect pests, and these sometimes kill useful insects, such as bees, too.

Ruby-tailed wasps live in Great Britain and are an endangered species.

Bee and wasp fact

Farmers in Africa are being taught how to keep honeybees. The bees pollinate the crops and also provide honey.

Female mason bees lay their eggs in the tiny tubes of nest boxes.

Bee conservation

People can help bees by putting special nest houses in their yards. Nest houses for a type of bee called a mason bee are made of lots of tiny tubes, and are placed on a wall or fence. Bumblebee nest houses are filled with a nesting material and placed on the ground.

Life cycle of a honeybee

Eggs are laid by the queen. After 3 days, larvae hatch out of the eggs. The larvae grow for up to 9 days and then turn into pupae. An adult honeybee emerges after about 10 days. Worker bees born in spring and summer live for about 6 weeks. Those born in the fall live through the winter. A queen lives for 2 to 3 years. Drones live for a few months.

Eggs

Larvae

Emerging adult

Glossary

abdomen third part of an insect's body, behind the thorax

antennae feelers that detect smells in the air

extinct not existing anymore, disappeared completely

habitat the place in which an animal or plant lives

host insect the insect on which a parasite lives or lays its eggs

insect animal with a head, thorax, abdomen, and three pairs of legs

larva (plural larvae) the growing stage between an egg and a pupa

mate to pair or breed

metamorphosis a change in appearance, such as when a larva changes into a bee

nectar the sugary liquid produced by many flowers

parasites animals that live on other animals

pollen a powder produced by flowers

predator an animal that hunts and kills other animals

prey an animal that is hunted by another animal

pupa (plural pupae) structure in which the body of the larva is rearranged into an adult

social living in a group with other insects or animals

solitary living alone, rather than as part of a group

thorax the second part of the body of an insect, joining the head to the abdomen

ultraviolet a color that cannot be seen by humans without a special light

vibrate to move back and forth in small, fast movements

Index

abdomen 4, 14, 17, 27, 31
antennae 18, 31

bee-eater 24
beekeeping 8
bees, differences between wasps and 5
beeswax 14
bumblebees 6, 8, 29
buzz pollinators 21
buzzing 20, 32

carpenter bees 21
cells 10, 13, 14, 15, 22
colonies 12–13
combs 14
common wasps 5, 7, 28
communication 26–27
conservation 29

dancing 27
digger wasps 7
drones 12, 30

eggs 5, 10, 14, 17, 30
extinct 28, 31
eyes 18

fairyfly 17
feelers (antennae) 18, 31
flight 20–21
food 10, 20, 22–23
foragers 13

habitat 8, 28, 31
hairs 5
hive 10
honey 10, 14, 22, 28
honey badger 24
honeybees 4, 5, 6, 8, 9, 10, 11, 12–13, 14, 20, 27, 28, 30
honey spoon 22
hornets 6, 7
host insect 17, 31
house bees 13

insects 4, 5, 23, 31
invertebrates 4

larva 5, 10–11, 14, 24, 30, 31
legs 4
life cycle 5, 30
lifespan 30

mason bees 29
mate 12, 31
metamorphosis 11, 31

nectar 8, 13, 22, 23, 31
nest houses 29
nests 14–15, 22
nurse bee 13

ovipositor 17

paper wasps 7
parasites 6, 7, 17, 18, 31
pesticides 28
pheromones 26
pollen 10, 13, 14, 21, 22, 31
pollen baskets 22
pollinators 21
potter wasps 7, 16
predator 24, 25, 31
prey 24, 31
pupa 5, 11, 14, 30, 31

queen 10, 12, 13, 15, 30

royal jelly 13
ruby-tailed wasps 28

senses 18–19
sight 18, 19
smell 18, 26, 27
social 6, 7, 12, 14, 31
solitary 6, 7, 16–17, 31
sting 4, 8, 9, 24, 25

thorax 4, 31
threats to bees and wasps 28–29
tongue 22
types of bees and wasps 6

ultraviolet 18, 19, 31

vibrate 21, 31

waist 5
warning colors 25
wasps, differences between bees and 5
wax 14
wings 4, 20, 21
workers 12, 13, 15, 22, 26, 30